# Who Works Here?

# Dental Office

by Lola M. Schaefer

Heinemann Library
Chicago, Illinois

© 2000 Reed Educational & Professional Publishing
Published by Heinemann Library,
an imprint of Reed Educational & Professional Publishing,
100 N. LaSalle, Suite 1010
Chicago, IL 60602
Customer Service  888-454-2279

Printed in Hong Kong
Designed by Made in Chicago Design Associates


04 03 02 01 00
10 9 8 7 6 5 4 3 2 1

**Library of Congress Cataloging-in-Publication Data**
Schaefer, Lola M., 1950
      Dental office / Lola Schaefer.
         p. cm.  – (Who works here?)
      Includes bibliographical references and index.
      Summary: Introduces some of the people who work at a dental office
   and the jobs they perform, including receptionist, dental hygienist,
   dental assistant, and dentist.
      ISBN  1-57572-517-7  (library binding)
      1. Dentistry Juvenile literature.  2. Children—Preparation for
   dental care.   3. Dental personnel Juvenile literature.
      [1. Dentistry  2. Dentists.  3. Dental care.   4. Occupations.]
      I. Title.   II. Series.
   RK63.S295   2000
   617.6—dc21                                           99-40760
                                                           CIP


**Acknowledgments**
All photographs by Phil Martin.

Special thanks to Dr. Robert Overdorf and his staff in St. Charles, Illinois, and to workers
everywhere who take pride in what they do.

Every effort has been made to contact copyright holders of any material reproduced in this book.
Any omissions will be rectified in subsequent printings if notice is given to the publisher.

Some words are shown in bold, **like this.**
You can find out what they mean by looking in the glossary.

# Contents

# What Is a Dental Office?

A dental office is a business where a dentist and staff care for **patients'** teeth. People of all ages make **appointments** at the dental office. Some patients have their teeth cleaned and others have their teeth repaired.

It is important to keep all **instruments** and exam rooms clean in a dental office. Everyone works together to keep the patient areas **disinfected.** Any instrument that is used needs to be **sterilized** before it is used with another patient. The dentist and staff wear rubber gloves to protect the patients and themselves.

This dental office is in St. Charles, Illinois. This floor plan shows all of the places where the people in this book are working. Many dental offices in the United States have similar floor plans.

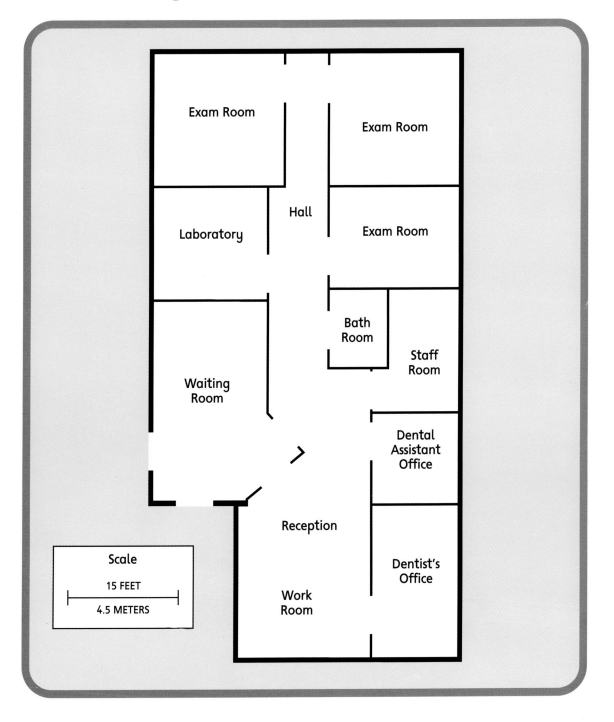

Exam Room

Exam Room

Hall

Laboratory

Exam Room

Bath Room

Staff Room

Waiting Room

Dental Assistant Office

Reception

Dentist's Office

Work Room

Scale
15 FEET
4.5 METERS

# Receptionist

A receptionist welcomes all visitors and makes **appointments** for **patients,** both in the office and over the telephone. Every day, the receptionist gives a typed list of patient appointments to the dentist and staff.

Mae is a receptionist. Here she helps a new patient fill out an information sheet.

Mae must enter information about the
patient into the office computer.

Like many receptionists, Mae went to secretarial school to
learn how to manage an office. As a secretary, she types
letters for the dentist and files patient charts. She mails
reminders for upcoming appointments. A receptionist keeps
the office **organized** and answers questions.

# Bookkeeper

Here, Mae receives a check from a **patient.**
As the bookkeeper, Mae will enter the check
amount into the computer.

Since many dental offices have small staffs, workers
have many jobs. In this office, Mae is also the
bookkeeper. The bookkeeper enters all charges and
payments on a computer. At the end of each month,
the bookkeeper sends reminders for unpaid bills.

The bookkeeper is responsible for recording all purchases and **fees** for the dentist. The furniture, **instruments,** and supplies in a dental office all cost money. The dentist pays himself or herself and the staff for their work. Each **patient** pays a fee for their dental care.

Mae pulls patient files to enter payments sent through the mail.

# Dental Hygienist

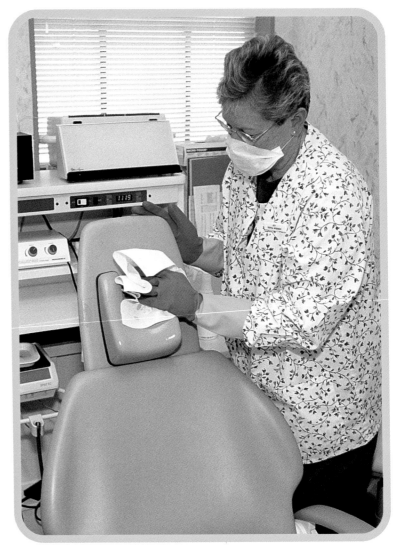

Joy is a dental hygienist. She must **disinfect** the headrest before each patient.

A dental hygienist helps the dentist take care of **patients**. During a visit, the dental hygienist cleans, polishes, and flosses the patient's teeth. Afterward, the dental hygienist asks the patient to use **fluoride** to make the outer covering of the teeth harder.

Joy, like many dental hygienists, went to college for three years. She studied the body, teeth, and how to use dental **instruments.** She learned how to work with patients and keep them comfortable. Dental hygienists learn new information at **conferences.**

The dental hygienist records any changes in the patient's health.

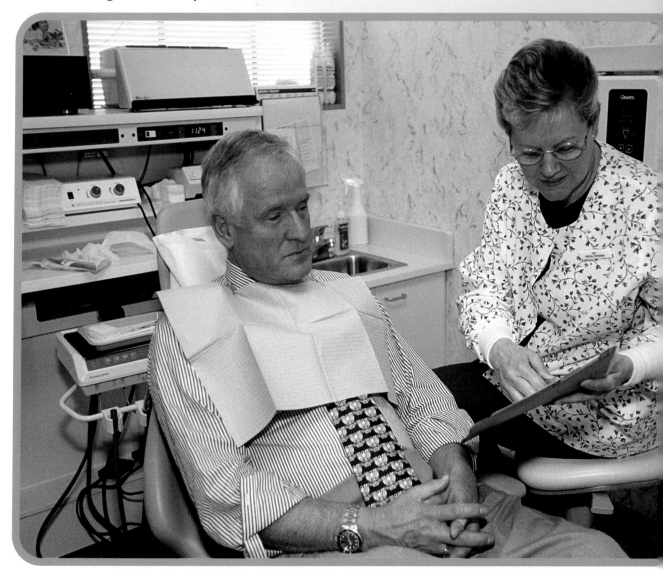

# Dental Hygienist and Instruments

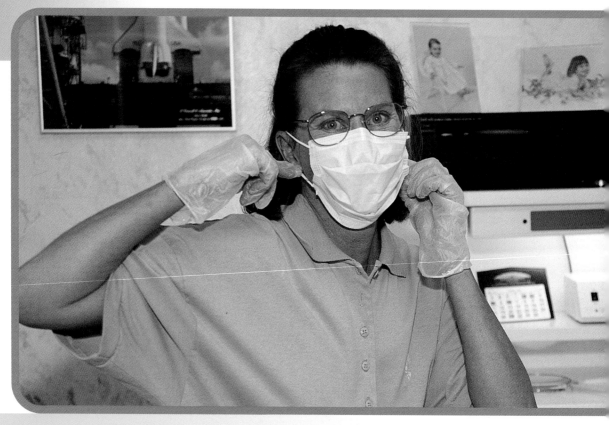

Carolyn, a dental hygienist, wears a face mask while working with patients. This helps to keep the patient and Carolyn from spreading harmful germs.

A dental hygienist uses different **instruments** as she or he cleans a **patient's** teeth. A scaler removes **tartar** from the teeth, both above and below the gum line. An explorer checks for **cavities**. A probe measures gum and bone health.

All dental hygienists teach their patients how to care for their own teeth. At each visit, they remind the patients to brush their teeth twice a day. They ask everyone to floss once a day. Dental hygienists show how important it is to clean in between the teeth.

Carolyn has just finished polishing this girl's teeth. Now they can share smiles.

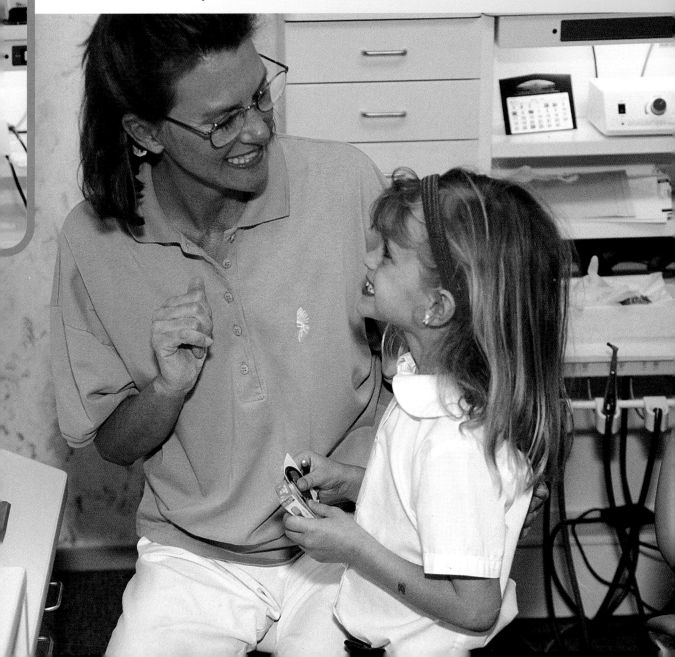

# Cleaning Instruments

After each dental treatment, the dental staff must **sterilize** all the **instruments**. In the lab, a staff member scrubs the instruments under water. Then, they are put into an **ultrasonic** cleaner for five minutes. It removes loose particles from the instruments.

The dental assistant cleans one set of instruments at a time.

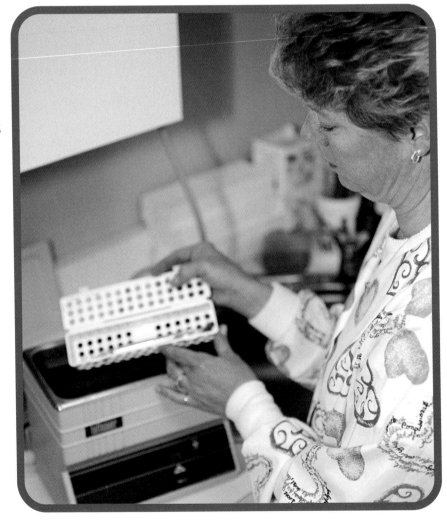

Each set of instruments is then put into a sterilizing pouch. The pouch is placed on a tray in the **autoclave**. Water inside the autoclave is heated and turns to steam. The instruments stay in the autoclave for 45 minutes.

The steam in the autoclave will kill all germs on the instruments.

# Dental Assistant

A dental assistant helps the dentist while working with a **patient**. The assistant hands **instruments** to the dentist and moves the patient's tongue or cheek out of the dentist's way. A dental assistant is responsible for mixing fillings.

Sally, a dental assistant, holds a special light while the dentist puts in a filling.

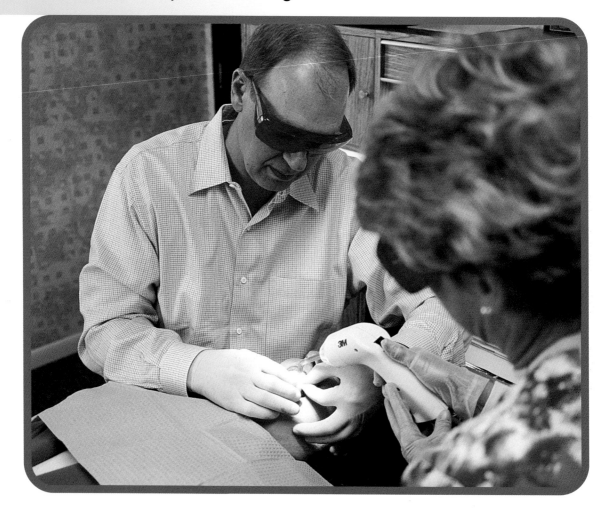

16

Sally, like most dental assistants, went to college for two years. Then, she spent another year in a college dental **clinic**. Today she is a **certified** dental assistant. The dentist and dental assistant attend **conferences** together to learn the latest ways of helping patients.

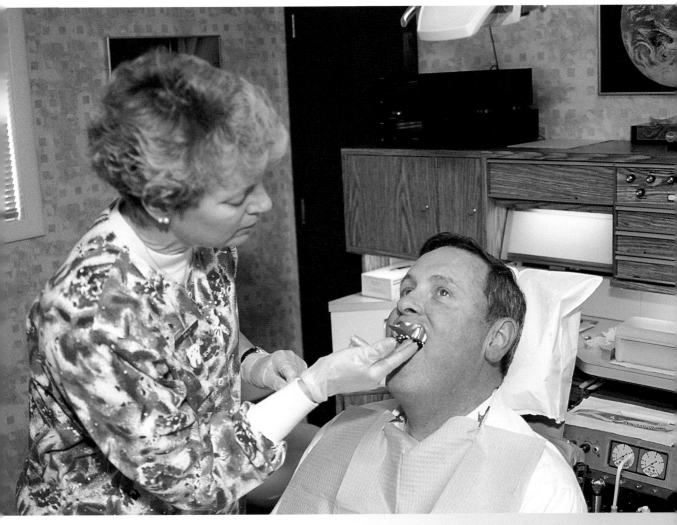

Sally makes an **impression** of a patient's mouth.

# Dental Assistant and Models

The dental assistant measures
carefully when making mixes.

Sometimes the dentist asks the dental assistant to make
a model of a **patient's** mouth. The dental assistant mixes
a soft material in a bowl and places it in a mouth tray.
The patient bites down and holds still while the
material becomes firm.

In the lab, the dental assistant pours plaster into the **mold.** She lets it set until it is hard. Later, she peels away the tray and a model of the patient's mouth remains. The dentist studies the model to decide what treatment the patient may need.

The plaster model is labeled with the patient's name and other important information.

# Dentist

Robb is a dentist who owns his own office.
Here, he and his staff discuss a patient's health file.

Many dentists own their own dental offices. Dentists want a friendly office where everyone works together to give the best care to all **patients.** Dentists hope that every patient will have their own strong teeth for as long as they live.

Most dentists go to college for four years and study **biology.** Afterwards, they spend four more years studying to become a dentist. Most dentists travel each year to dental meetings. They also learn new information from **journals** and newsletters.

Between **appointments,** Robb reads newsletters about dentistry in his office.

# Dentist and Patients

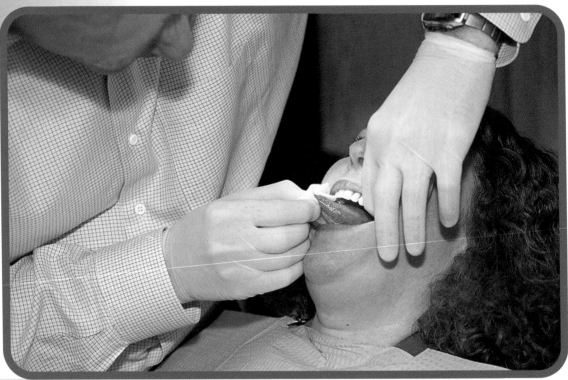

Robb always gives each patient an **oral cancer** check.

Most dentists enjoy working with **patients.** Sometimes they must put a filling in a tooth. If a patient has an accident, the dentist must repair teeth. Some patients need their teeth sealed. The dentist puts a plastic covering over the teeth. This prevents food from collecting in pits and grooves, which can cause a **cavity.**

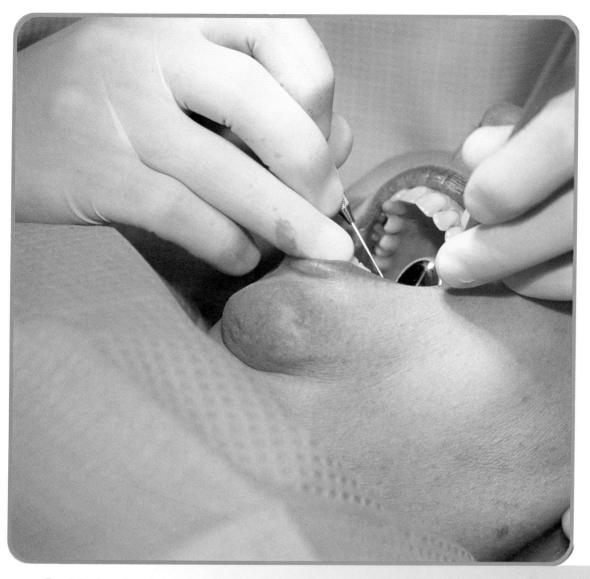

Robb looks for changes in a patient's mouth.

The dentist and his staff need to know their patients' past health. They ask about their present health habits. The dentist warns patients about habits that will injure their teeth. He asks them not to smoke or eat foods with a lot of sugar.

# Dentist and X-rays

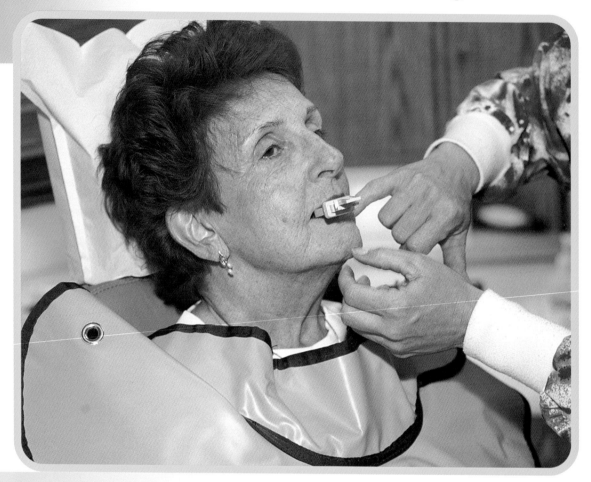

The dental assistant puts x-ray
film into a patient's mouth.

When a dentist looks into a **patient's** mouth, he can
see the teeth and gums. But to see the root of the
tooth, or the jawbone, the dentist needs to see x-rays.
The dental assistant or dental hygienist is trained
to take x-rays of the teeth and mouth.

The dental assistant puts a **lead** apron across the patient. This protects the patient's body from the x-ray beam. After the film is in the patient's mouth, the head of the x-ray machine is put into position. Then, the picture is taken.

The x-ray machine is placed within inches of the patient's mouth to take the picture.

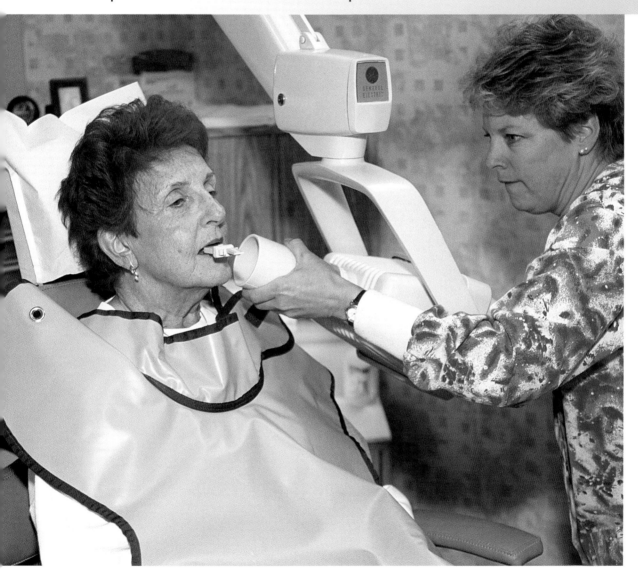

# Reading the X-rays

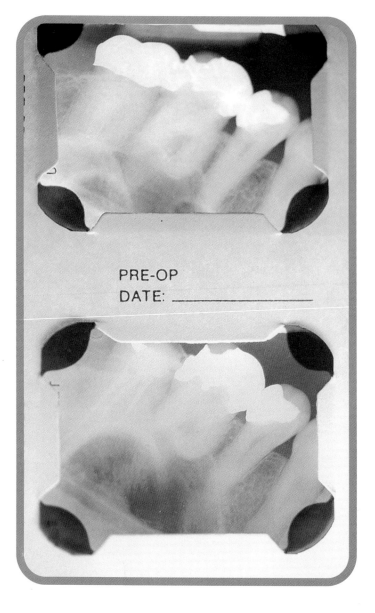

PRE-OP
DATE: _____

X-rays show the tooth and tissue above and below the gum line.

The dentist is able to look at the **patients'** x-rays three minutes after the picture is taken. The film is **developed** in the dental office by the dental assistant or hygienist. Each slide is labeled with the date and patient's name.

Once the dentist has the x-ray pictures, he puts them on a light board. He studies each one carefully. He notes which teeth are healthy and which teeth need repair. Sometimes the dentist shows the patient the x-rays so they can discuss treatment.

Here, Robb marks a patient's x-rays to discuss treatment.

# Dental Office Staff

The dental hygienists and the dental assistant meet with the dentist at the beginning of each day. They look at the list of **appointments**. They discuss any **patients** that may have special needs. The staff works hard so all patients receive the best care.

A dental hygienist removes **tartar** from a boy's teeth.

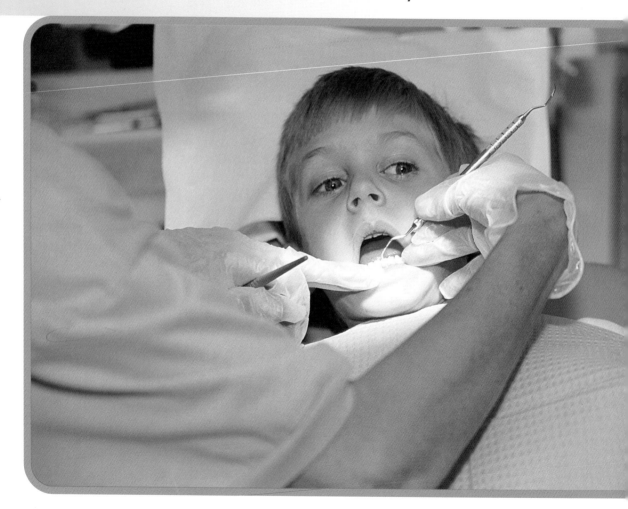

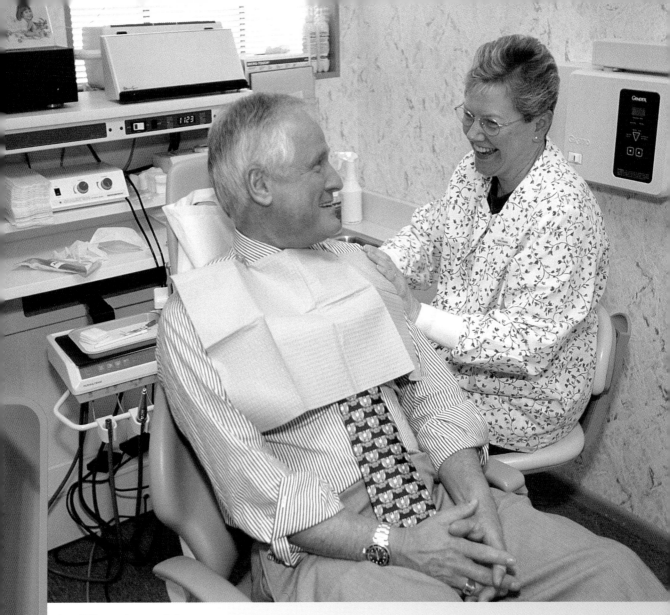

The dental hygienist explains the
treatment before she begins.

Each staff member works with patients every day.
Everyone in the office must work well with people. The
dentist wants the staff to be helpful and friendly. Above
all, the dentist wants the staff to show concern for the
well-being of every patient.

# Glossary

**appointment** time agreed for a meeting

**autoclave** electric machine that uses steam to kill germs on dental and medical tools

**biology** science that studies living things

**cavity** hole in a tooth caused by decay

**certified** licensed to perform a job after passing a test proving knowledge of important information

**clinic** place that gives medical or dental treatment

**conference** meeting of people in which ideas and information are shared

**developed** treated with chemicals to bring out the picture that is on the film

**disinfected** cleaned with a product that kills germs

**fee** money that is paid for a service

**fluoride** mixture of chemicals that strengthens teeth

**impression** exact copy of something

**instrument** tool for scientific work

**journal** newspaper or magazine that gives new information to its readers

**lead** very heavy but soft, gray metal; x-rays cannot pass through lead mold  hollow form that gives a special shape when filled with liquid or soft material

oral cancer  very serious disease that is found in the mouth of people

organized  arranged neatly and kept in order

patient  person who is being treated by a doctor or dentist

sterilized  cleaned and not having any germs

tartar  hard crust that can form on teeth when food is not cleaned away

ultrasonic  using the vibrations of high-frequency sound waves

# More Books to Read

Flanagan, Alice K. *Dr. Kanner, Dentist with a Smile.* New York: Children's Press, 1997.

Johnston, Marianne. *Let's Talk About Going to the Dentist.* New York: PowerKids Press, 1997.

Kessel, Joyce K. *Careers: Dental Care.* Minneapolis, Minn.: Lerner Publications, 1984.

Ready, Dee. *Dentists.* Mankato, Minn.: Bridgestone Books, 1998.

# Index